Weird America!

AMERICA'S ODDEST LANDMARKS

By Sarah Machajewski

Gareth Stevens
PUBLISHING

Please visit our website, www.garethstevens.com. For a free color catalog of all our high-quality books, call toll free 1-800-542-2595 or fax 1-877-542-2596.

Library of Congress Cataloging-in-Publication Data

Names: Machajewski, Sarah, author.
Title: America's oddest landmarks / Sarah Machajewski.
Description: New York : Gareth Stevens Publishing, 2016. | Series: Weird
   America | Includes index.
Identifiers: LCCN 2015030540 | ISBN 9781482440232 (pbk.) | ISBN 9781482440249
   (6 pack) | ISBN 9781482440256 (library bound)
Subjects: LCSH: United States–Description and travel–Miscellanea. |
   Curiosities and wonders–United States. | Public sculpture, American.
Classification: LCC E169.Z83 M27 2016 | DDC 917.304–dc 3
LC record available at http://lccn.loc.gov/2015030540

First Edition

Published in 2016 by
Gareth Stevens Publishing
111 East 14th Street, Suite 349
New York, NY 10003

Copyright © 2016 Gareth Stevens Publishing

Designer: Sarah Liddell
Editor: Ryan Nagelhout

Photo credits: Cover, p. 1 (arrow) Mascha Tace/Shutterstock.com; cover, p. 1 Ionas Kaltenbach/Lonely Planet Images/
Getty Images; sidebar used throughout zayats-and-zayats/Shutterstock.com; background texture used throughout
multipear/Shutterstock.com; p. 5 Sanjay ach/Wikimedia Commons; p. 7 George Rose/Contributor/Getty Images
Entertainment/Getty Images; p. 9 Felix Mizioznikov/Shutterstock.com; p. 11 TheWhitePelican/Wikimedia Commons;
p. 12 Melissa Mahoney/Contributor/Moment Mobile/Getty Images; p. 13 Kosei Saito/Contributor/Moment/
Getty Images; pp. 14, 15 (main) Education Images/Contributor/Universal Images Group/Getty Images;
p. 15 (Stonehenge) aslysun/Shutterstock.com; p. 16 Hayati Kayhan/Shutterstock.com; p. 17 TigerPaw2154/
Wikimedia Commons; p. 18 CarolSpears/Wikimedia Commons; p. 19 (pistachio) Mike Theiss/Contributor/National
Geographic/Getty Images; p. 19 (artichoke) Maureen Sullivan/Contributor/Moment Mobile/Getty Images;
p. 19 (chess piece) Dilip Vishwanat/Stringer/Getty Images Group/Getty Images; p. 19 (roller skate) Laura Kalcheff/
Contributor/Moment Mobile/Getty Images; p. 19 (thermometer) Jason Kirk/Staff/Hulton Archive/Getty Images;
p. 20 Sarah Fields Photography/Shutterstock.com; p. 21 Daderot/Wikimedia Commons; p. 22 Walter Bibikow/
Photolibrary/Getty Images; p. 23 Cory Doctorow/Flickr.com; p. 24 Lynne Gilbert/Contributor/Moment Mobile/
Getty Images; p. 25 (Lucy) Cocoruff/Wikimedia Commons; p. 25 (Lenny) Portland Press Herald/Contributor/Portland
Press Herald/Getty Images; p. 26 Andreas Feininger/Contributor/The LIFE PIcture Collection/Getty Images;
p. 27 Scott Olson/Staff/Getty Images News/Getty Images; p. 29 Bill Hinton/Contributor/Moment Mobile/Getty Images.

Printed in the United States of America

CPSIA compliance information: Batch #CW16GS: For further information contact Gareth Stevens, New York, New York at 1-800-542-2595.

CONTENTS

Words in the glossary appear in **bold** type the first time they are used in the text.

WEIRD FROM COAST TO COAST

Mount Rushmore. The Statue of Liberty. The Grand Canyon. What do these places have in common? They're American landmarks. Landmarks are structures, objects, or features of unusual interest. They're easy to recognize, and people love to visit them.

Landmarks are often famous for being historically or **geographically** important. But the United States is also full of landmarks that are truly weird. In between coasts, you'll find man-made things as odd as the biggest ball of twine and as naturally weird as a desert in the coastal state of Maine. But no matter what the landmarks are, one thing's for sure—they're all **uniquely** American.

Not Your Average Landmark

The United States has more than 2,500 National Historic Landmarks. These are landmarks that represent the history and people of the United States, such as San Francisco's Golden Gate Bridge and St. Louis's Gateway Arch. Some of the landmarks in this book are on this list. Others are too weird to make the list!

4

ENTRANCE To MYSTERY SPOT ●

OPEN

PLEASE SMOKE

50¢

SANTA CRUZ

The Mystery Spot near Santa Cruz, California, opened in 1941. It's one of many weird attractions scattered throughout the United States.

GREETINGS FROM "BLUCIFER"

The Denver International Airport saw 53.4 million travelers pass through in 2014. While they may have arrived in Colorado expecting to see the Rocky Mountains, a 32-foot (9.8 m) blue horse greeted them instead.

Blue Mustang is the official name for the 9,000-pound (4,082 kg) horse statue that stands outside the Denver airport. Beyond its paint job, people can't help but notice the mustang's fiery red eyes and angry look—something so odd, it's earned the horse the nickname "Blucifer," after Lucifer, another name for the devil. Since 2008, it has inspired **controversy**. Some people think the mustang is too creepy, but it's impossible to miss.

Cursed?

Blue Mustang's looks aren't the only reason for its creepy reputation. On June 13, 2006, three sections of the sculpture came loose and fell on its creator, Luis Jiménez! The accident cut an **artery** in Jiménez's leg, killing him. Many people feel the horse has been cursed ever since.

Blue Mustang was made
to symbolize, or stand for, the
wild spirit of the American West.
But many people think it symbolizes
something far more evil.

7

RACETRACK MYTHOLOGY

Americans may have a thing for giant horse sculptures. In Hallandale Beach, Florida, a horse statue 110 feet (33.5 m) tall towers over the Gulfstream Park racetrack. If that isn't strange enough, the horse has giant wings and appears to be stepping on a dragon with its big steel hoof. The horse and dragon are taken straight from Greek **mythology**, after the story of Pegasus, the flying horse.

This gigantic landmark is made of 440 tons (399 mt) of steel and 220 tons (200 mt) of bronze. The statue has created buzz among residents and visitors to Gulfstream Park. It's not uncommon to see people trying to get a picture with the huge mythological creatures!

Attracting the Public

Gulfstream Park has big plans for its Pegasus statue. They want to turn it from a single landmark into an entire park. The statue currently stands over a dome that one day may become a theater, and city officials plan to add landscaping and a giant waterfall around it. Gulfstream Park officials hope this odd landmark will one day become "the Eiffel Tower of Hallandale Beach."

8

Gulfstream Park is a racetrack for real horses. Today, they race in the shadow of this $30 million giant landmark.

9

A WHALE ON ROUTE 66

Few of us may ever see a whale in person—unless you take Route 66 through Catoosa, Oklahoma. In the late 1960s, a man named Hugh Davis had a dream about a giant whale in a pond where his grandchildren swam and played.

Davis and a friend built the big beast, which ended up being 20 feet (6.1 m) tall and 80 feet (24.4 m) long. When it was completed in 1972, Davis's grandchildren weren't the only people to enjoy "Ol' Blue." People jumped off its tail, slid down its fins, and walked through its mouth! Today, thousands of travelers a year visit this fun roadside attraction.

The Mother Road

US Highway 66 is about as American as the odd landmarks and attractions that dot its path. Created in 1926, Route 66 wove through eight states, connecting Chicago, Illinois, and Los Angeles, California. Route 66 has been replaced in the highway system, but it holds a special place in history as a reminder of the United States' spirited past.

Ol' Blue isn't the only odd American landmark along the old Route 66. Some of the other landmarks discussed in this book are located there, too.

CADILLAC RANCH

Cars are a true symbol of America. What better way to celebrate them than placing them nose down in the dirt? Welcome to Cadillac Ranch, a work of art near Amarillo, Texas, that has become one of the oddest landmarks in the United States.

Cadillac Ranch was built in 1974 by a group of artists known as the Ant Farm. Backed by billionaire Stanley Marsh 3, the artists bought 10 Cadillac cars from junkyards and buried them nose down in the ground, leaning at an angle.

Today, the Cadillacs look much different than they did in 1974. Travelers who stop to see the oddity add to the art by carving their name into the cars or spray-painting them crazy colors!

The Changing Cadillac

The cars at Cadillac Ranch are repainted quite often. In 2002, they were **restored** to their original colors. In 2003, they were painted black to honor the death of one of the founding members of the Ant Farm. But the paint jobs don't last long—it's only a matter of time before new travelers show up with some spray paint.

Cadillac Ranch is off Route 66, west of Amarillo. Visitors are encouraged to leave their mark on the cars, but stealing from or harming the cars isn't allowed.

A MONUMENT OF CARS

Stonehenge is a **prehistoric** monument in England and is often considered one of the Seven Wonders of the World. The United States has its own **version** of it, but it's made of cars!

Carhenge in Alliance, Nebraska, is an unusual landmark that came about in 1987 after the death of the artist's father. Jim Reinders arranged 39 cars in the shape and size of Stonehenge. Some cars are buried in the ground, while others form the structure's mysterious arches. The cars are painted gray to resemble the stones at Stonehenge. More than 60,000 people visit this odd landmark each year.

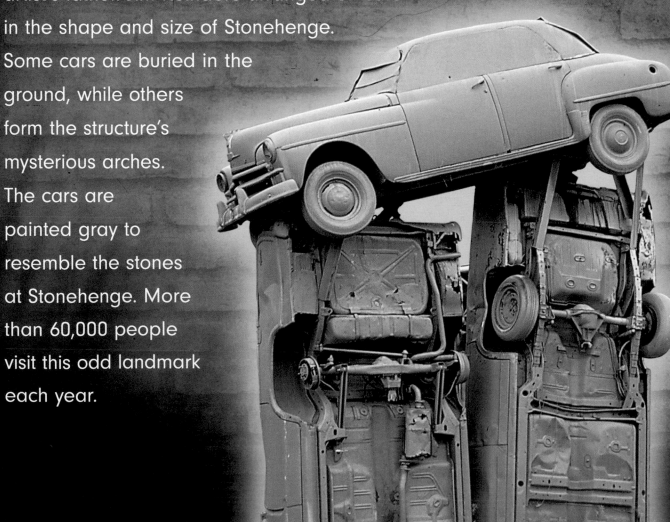

Here Lie Foreign Cars

Carhenge is about as American as it gets. The original sculpture was built with three cars not built in America. They were, however, removed and replaced with cars built in the United States. In the spirit of the mysterious Stonehenge, the cars were buried near Carhenge during a "ritual."

Carhenge is arranged in a circle that measures 96 feet (29.3 m) across, just like Stonehenge.

Stonehenge

15

THE WORLD'S LARGEST...

What would you do with a ball of twine that measures 41.4 feet (12.6 m) around, 8 feet (2.4 m) across, and almost 11 feet (3.4 m) high? Turn it into a roadside **tourist** attraction, of course!

In 1953, Frank Stoeber of Cawker City, Kansas, started winding spare twine into a ball. After 4 years, it weighed over 5,000 pounds (2,268 kg)! By 1961, Stoeber had wound more than 1.6 million feet (487,680 m) of twine into a giant ball. He gave it to the town that same year, and it's been growing ever since. Today, it holds the title of the World's Largest Ball of Twine that's been built by a community.

Another Ball of Twine

A few hundred miles away from Cawker City sits Twine II. Francis Johnson from Darwin, Minnesota, started wrapping a ball of twine in 1950. He added twine every day for 29 years. It's 12 feet (3.7 m) across, weighs 17,400 pounds (7,893 kg), and is the largest ball of twine wrapped by a single person.

Visitors can wrap their own twine around the ball when they come to Cawker City. A "Twine-a-Thon" is held every third Saturday in August. That way, residents and visitors alike help the World's Largest Ball of Twine keep its title.

17

Of course, balls of twine aren't the only landmarks that are considered the "world's largest." Visitors to Cottonwood, Idaho, can spend the night inside the world's largest beagle. The Dog Bark Park Inn is a bed-and-breakfast built in the shape of the owners' favorite animal!

In Red Wing, Minnesota, the world's largest boot stands at 16 feet (4.9 m) tall and weighs over 2,000 pounds (907 kg). It's said the boot is too big for the Statue of Liberty to wear! And, if you like ketchup, you might want to visit the world's largest bottle in Collinsville, Illinois. The 170-foot (51.8 m) "ketchup bottle" is actually a water tower that could hold nearly 70,312.5 gallons (266,161.8 L) of water—or ketchup.

The Largest in America

Here are a few more of the world's largest landmarks that can be found around America: World's Largest Light Bulb (Edison, New Jersey); World's Largest Santa Claus (North Pole, Alaska); World's Largest Penny (Woodruff, Wisconsin); World's Largest Baseball Bat (Louisville, Kentucky).

THE LARGEST THINGS ON EARTH

largest
artichoke
Castroville,
California

largest
pistachio
Alamogordo,
New Mexico,

largest
roller skate
Warrenton,
Virginia

largest
chess piece
St. Louis,
Missouri

largest
thermometer
Baker,
California

19

NATURE'S WEIRD WONDERS

Sometimes nature creates landmarks that are just as odd as the ones made by people. The Desert of Maine near Freeport, Maine, was created more than 11,000 years ago during the end of the last **ice age**. A glacier moved over the area and left behind glacial silt, a material that's finer than sand.

Despite what its name says, this landmark isn't a true desert because it gets a lot of rain. But to the more than 30,000 visitors who see it each year, the wide, sandy "desert" in the middle of Maine is a big surprise!

Balanced Rock in Garden of the Gods

Rocky Gods

If you ever visit Colorado Springs, Colorado, be sure to visit the Garden of the Gods. This national landmark features sandstone rocks that stand more than 300 feet (91 m) high. The red rocks were shaped over millions of years by rock movement and **erosion**, which made very strange shapes. One rock even looks like it's balancing on another.

Nature has the power to create weird, yet beautiful, landmarks all on its own.

Desert of Maine

Americans love to pay **tribute** to presidents, sometimes in odd ways. President Jimmy Carter was known for his past as a peanut farmer and his toothy smile. In 1976, three residents of Evanston, Indiana, combined both into a smiling peanut statue. This landmark currently stands near Carter's hometown of Plains, Georgia.

After visiting the famous Mount Rushmore in South Dakota, artist David Adickes set out to make giant heads of each president for himself. Visitors to Pearland, Texas, can climb on and touch the statues. Some tourists like to pick the presidents' noses!

smiling peanut statue

Adickes said he was disappointed visitors couldn't actually touch and see the presidents' heads up close at Mount Rushmore, so he made his own presidential heads.

Stone Faces

At the Mount Rushmore National Memorial, visitors can see the stone likenesses of Thomas Jefferson, Abraham Lincoln, George Washington, and Theodore Roosevelt looking over the Black Hills of South Dakota. Just over 16 miles (26 km) away, only the face has been completed on a giant monument to honor the great Native American leader Crazy Horse.

23

BIG, BIG ANIMALS

Did you know the world's largest elephant stands over six stories tall? Her name is Lucy, and she's over 130 years old. This national landmark in Atlantic City, New Jersey, is made of wood and tin, and weighs about 90 tons (82 mt). Throughout history, Lucy has been used as an office, a restaurant, and a bar!

Another animal oddity is Lenny the Chocolate Moose. Made of 1,700 pounds (771 kg) of pure milk chocolate, Lenny is one of a kind. No need to worry about him melting—his room at his chocolate-shop home in Maine never gets above 70°F (21°C).

Dinny

Dino Days

If you've ever wanted to see a dinosaur, there are some odd landmarks that can help you out. Dinosaur Park in South Dakota has five dinosaurs that greet you on your way to Mount Rushmore. Or meet Dinny the Dinosaur at Cabazon Dinosaurs in California. He's a brontosaurus that's also a building!

Lucy

People love animals,
especially when they're huge
and made of chocolate!

Lenny

25

OUT-OF-BODY ODDITIES

Body parts are usually meant to stay where they belong, but in the case of landmarks, anything goes. If you've lost a tooth, you might want to look for it in Trenton, New Jersey. There, the world's largest tooth stands near train tracks that pass through the city.

In 2010, Chicago welcomed a 30-foot (9.1 m) eyeball in its downtown Pritzker Park. The sculpture has moved since then, and tourists can now see it in Dallas, Texas, where it was installed in 2013. No matter where it is, visitors can agree this odd—and maybe a bit creepy—landmark is definitely a sight to see.

Paul Bunyan

Larger Than Life

The giant eyeball and giant tooth could belong to any of the landmarks that have turned normal-sized people into giants. From Paul Bunyan and his blue ox in Minnesota to the Lady in the Lake in Alabama, many of the oddest attractions are people that have become larger than life.

Artist Tony Tasset's giant eyeball sculpture stands out no matter what city it's visiting.

27

A SHARED EXPERIENCE

The landmarks we've covered in this book may seem silly, strange, weird, or just plain freaky. They're all those things, but they're also tied to the unique spirit of America. Roadside attractions began appearing after the United States developed its highways.

For the first time, people were able to travel long distances around the country by car. They didn't just see the United States' beautiful geography, but the weird creations people whipped up to bring tourists to them. Over time, visiting the landmarks became just another part of America. Maybe one day you can see them, too!

Hit the Road!

The only way to truly experience these odd landmarks is to see them yourself. You can start small by looking for weird places to visit near your hometown. If you're going on a family trip, do some studying and take a look at a map. Are there any of these weird attractions you can see along the way?

The Fremont Troll in
Seattle, Washington, sits
under the George Washington
Memorial Bridge holding a
real Volkswagen Beetle
in its hand!

29

GLOSSARY

artery: a tube that carries blood from the heart to other body parts

controversy: a disagreement

erosion: the wearing away of matter by elements over a period of time

geographically: relating to location

ice age: a long period of cold and ice throughout Earth

mythology: a collection of myths, or stories, especially when belonging to a certain culture

prehistoric: having to do with a time before written records were kept

reputation: a widely held belief about someone or something

restore: to bring back to how something was before

ritual: relating to a religious or solemn ceremony

tourist: a person who travels or visits a place for fun

tribute: an act that is meant to show respect for someone or something

uniquely: in a manner different from other things

version: a particular form of something

FOR MORE INFORMATION

BOOKS

Boyer, Crispin. *National Geographic Kids Ultimate U.S. Road Trip Atlas.* Washington, DC: National Geographic, 2012.

Petruccio, Steven James. *Roadside Attractions Coloring Book: Weird and Wacky Landmarks from Across the USA!* Mineola, NY: Dover Books, 2012.

WEBSITES

American Landmarks
kidport.com/reflib/socialstudies/landmarks/Landmarks.htm
Find out more about some of the most famous American landmarks here.

Pit Stops for Kids
pitstopsforkids.com/category/pit-stop-2/roadside-attractions
Find more fun roadside pit stops around the country here.

Roadside America
roadsideamerica.com
Find some of the crazier American landmarks on this site.

INDEX